GELATIN

SHOT

RECIPES

Mom Never Made

It Like THIS!

Volume 1

By: Lisa Frank, Sheila Eineichner, and
Linnette Martin

GELATIN SHOT RECIPES

Mom Never Made It Like THIS!

Volume 1

Lisa Frank, Sheila Eineichner, and Linnette Martin

ISBN 978-1-4116-1695-0

Layout & cover work: Lisa Frank
Printing & publication: Lulu.com
Website: www.lulu.com/spotlight/leezil

Table Of Contents

Foreword

Here are some basic directions for making gelatin shots.

When making the shots, remember that the basic recipe is 1 cup of boiling liquid, 1 small (3oz) box of gelatin and 1 cup of cold liquid. Do not use straight alcohol, or the gelatin shots will not completely set. To the boiling liquid, slowly add the gelatin and stir for 2 minutes before adding the cold liquid.

The boiling liquid can be water, juice or soda. For the cold liquid, you can use water, juice, soda or alcohol.

If the recipe calls for dark, gold, light or flavored rum and you only have one type, feel free to use what you have.

One batch makes approximately 18-30 shots depending on the size soufflé cup used. Soufflé cups and lids can be purchased at most bulk supply stores.

1oz cup = 18-22 shots per batch
3/4oz cup = 26-30 shots per batch

Have fun with these recipes! We know we did!

Amaretto Sour

1c. Boiling Water
1 box Lemon Gelatin
2/3c. Amaretto
1/3c. Water

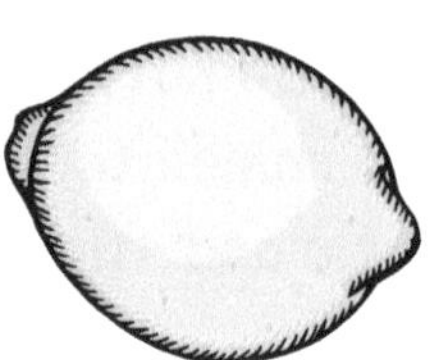

Angel Rouge

1c. Boiling Water
1 box Raspberry Gelatin
1/4c. Raspberry Vodka
1/4c. Blue Curacao
1/4c. Brandy
1/4c. Water

Angel's Tit

1c. Boiling Water
1 box Cherry Gelatin
1/3c. Cream De Cacao
1/3c. Half and Half
1/3c. Water

Place a chocolate chip on top when shot starts to set

Asian Orange

1c. Boiling Lemon-Lime Soda
1 box Sparkling Mandarin Orange Gelatin
1c. Orange Rum Flavored Malt Beverage

Bahama Mama

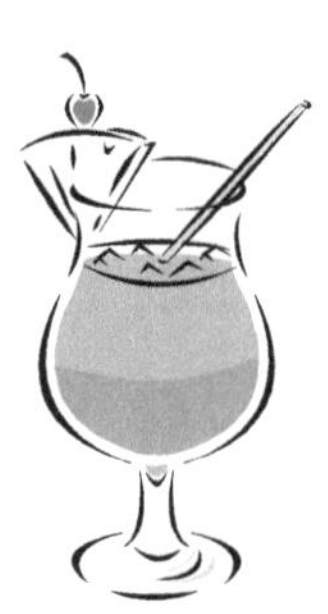

1c. Boiling Water
1 box Pineapple Gelatin
1/8c. Coconut Rum
1/8c. Dark Rum
1/2oz. Light Rum
1/2oz. Coffee Liqueur
5/8c. Orange Juice

Banana Split

1c. Boiling Water
1 box Strawberry-Banana Gelatin
1/4c. Strawberry Vodka
1/4c. Chocolate Liqueur
1/4c. Banana Liqueur
1/4c. Water

Place a Maraschino Cherry in the bottom of each cup

Berry Spritzer

1c. Boiled Lemon-Lime Soda
1 box Wild Berry Gelatin
1/3c. Strawberry Vodka
1/3c. Raspberry Schnapps
1/3c. Water

Blizzard

1c. Boiling Cranberry Juice
1 box Lemon Gelatin
2/3c. Bourbon
1/3c. Water

Blue Angel

1c. Boiling Water
1 box Berry Blue Gelatin
1/4c. Vanilla Vodka
3/8c. Blue Curacao
1/8c. Brandy
1/4c. Water

Blue Hooter

1c. Boiling Water
1 box Berry Blue Gelatin
1/3c. Watermelon Schnapps
1/3c. Blue Schnapps
1/3c. Water

Cappy and Cola

1c. Boiling Cola
1 box Lemon Gelatin
2/3c. Spiced Rum
1/3c. Cola

Caramel Apple

1c. Boiling Water
1 box Green Apple Gelatin
5/8c. Sour Apple Schnapps
1/8c. Butterscotch Schnapps
1/4c. Water

Caribbean Blue Blast

1c. Boiling Water
1 box Berry Blue Gelatin
1/2c. Coconut Rum
1/4c. Blue Schnapps
1/4c. Water

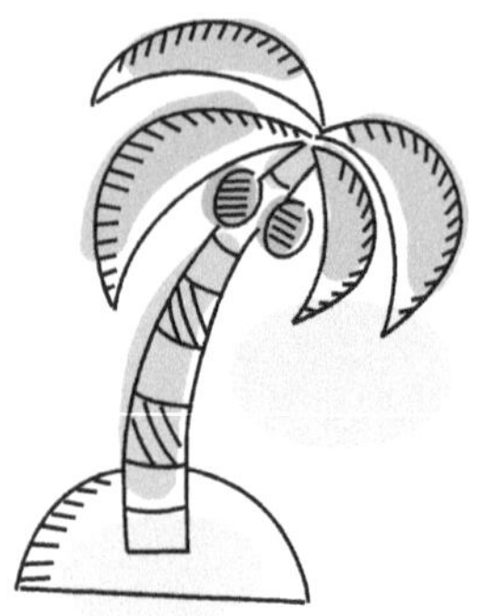

Casablanca

1c. Boiling Water
1 box Cherry Gelatin
1/2c. Light Rum
1/8c. Triple Sec
1/8c. Lime Juice
1/4c. Water

Place a Maraschino Cherry in the bottom of each cup

Champagne Fountain

1c. Boiling Water
1 box Sparkling Berry Gelatin
2/3c. Champagne
1/3c. Water

Cherry Poppin' Good

1c. Boiling Water
1 box Cherry Gelatin
2/3c. Amaretto
1/3c. Water

Chocolate Covered Cherry

1c. Boiling Water
1 box Cherry Gelatin
1/3c. Chocolate Liqueur
1/3c. Vanilla Vodka
1/3c. Water

Place a Maraschino Cherry in the bottom of each cup

Chocolate Raspberry Truffle

1c. Boiling Water
1 box Raspberry Gelatin
1/3c. Raspberry Liqueur
1/3c. Chocolate Liqueur
1/3c. Water

Coconut Craziness

1c. Boiling Water
1 box Pineapple Gelatin
2/3c. Coconut Rum
1/3c. Water

Cola Cerise

1c. Boiling Cola
1 box Cherry Gelatin
2/3c. Vanilla Vodka
1/3c. Cola

Cosmopolitan

5/8c. Boiling Water w/ 1/8c. Lime Juice
1 box Cranberry Gelatin
1/2c. Vodka
1/4c. Triple Sec
1/4c. Cranberry Juice

Fuzzy Martini

1c. Boiling Water
1 box Peach Gelatin
1/8c. Coffee Liqueur
3/8c. Vodka
1/4c. Peach Schnapps
1/4c. Water

Fuzzy Navel

1c. Boiling Water
1 box Orange Gelatin
1/2c. Peach Schnapps
1/2c. Water

Granny Never Had It So Good

1c. Boiling Water
1 box Green Apple Gelatin
2/3c. Sour Apple Schnapps
1/3c. Water

Grape Explosion

1c. Boiling Water
1 box Grape Gelatin
1/3c. Light Rum
1/3c. Grape Schnapps
1/3c. Water

Hair Raizer

1c. Boiling Rock and Rye Soda
1 box Cherry Gelatin
2/3c. Strawberry Vodka
1/3c. Rock and Rye Soda

Kamikaze

1c. Boiling Water
1 box Lime Gelatin
1/8c. Triple Sec
1/2c. Vodka
3/8c. Water

Lemon Drop

1c. Boiling Water
1 box Lemon Gelatin
2/3c. Vodka
1/3c. Lemonade

Long Island Iced Tea

1c. Boiling Cola
1 box Lemon Gelatin
2oz. Vodka
1oz. Gin
1oz. Light Rum
1oz. Tequila
1/2oz. Triple Sec
2-1/2oz. Water

Melon Ball

1c. Boiling Water
1 box Pineapple Gelatin
1/3c. Vodka
1/3c. Melon Liqueur
1/3c. Water

Nutty Colada

1c. Boiling Water
1 box Pineapple Gelatin
1/8c. Coconut Rum
1/8c. Gold Rum
3/8c. Amaretto
3/8c. Water

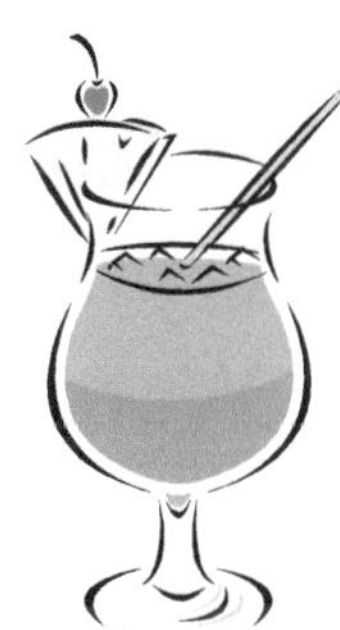

Orange Spritzer

1c. Boiling Lemon-Lime Soda
1 box Orange Gelatin
2/3c. Orange Rum
1/3c. Water

Peach Daiquiri

1c. Boiling Water w/ a Dash of Lime Juice
1 box Peach Gelatin
1/3c. Peach Schnapps
1/3c. Light Rum
1/3c. Water

Piña Colada

1c. Boiling Water
1 box Pineapple Gelatin
1/8c. Dark Rum
1/4c. Light Rum
1/4c. Coconut Rum
3/8c. Pineapple Juice

Purple Hooter

1c. Boiling Water
1 box Cranberry Gelatin
1/3c. Raspberry Liqueur
1/3c. Vodka
1/3c. Water

Purple Passion

1c. Boiling Water
1 box Grape Gelatin
1/3c. Amaretto
1/3c. Vodka
1/3c. Water

Raspberry Daiquiri

1c. boiling Water w/ a Dash of Lime Juice
1 box Raspberry Gelatin
1/3c. Raspberry Rum
1/3c. Raspberry Schnapps
1/3c. Water

Red Headed Slut

1c. Boiling Water
1 box Cranberry Gelatin
1/3c. Jagermeister®
1/3c. Southern Comfort®
1/3c. Cranberry Juice

Russian Rose

1c. Boiling Strawberry Soda
1 box Strawberry Gelatin
1/2c. Strawberry Vodka
1/8c. Dry Vermouth
1/8c. Grenadine
1/4c. Water

Scarlett O'Hara

1c. Boiling Cranberry Juice
1 box Lime Gelatin
1/2c. Southern Comfort®
1/2c. Water

Screwdriver

1c. Boiling Water
1 box Orange Gelatin
1/2c. Vodka
1/2c. Orange Juice

Sex on the Beach

1c. Boiling Cranberry Juice
1 box Pineapple Gelatin
1/3c. Vodka
1/3c. Peach Schnapps
1/3c. Water

Sicilian Kiss

1c. Boiling Water
1 box Lime Gelatin
1/3c. Southern Comfort®
1/3c. Amaretto
1/3c. Water

Strawberry-Banana Blitz

1c. Boiling Water
1 box Strawberry-Banana Gelatin
1/4c. Banana Rum
1/4c. Banana Liqueur
1/2c. Water

Swamp Water

1c. Boiling Water
1 box Lemon Gelatin
1/4c. Blue Curacao
1/2c. Dark Rum
1/4c. Orange Juice

Tequila Sunrise

1c. Boiling Water
1 box Orange Gelatin
1/2c. Tequila
1/8c. Grenadine
3/8c. Water

Those Steel Drums

1c. Boiling Water
1 box Berry Blue Gelatin
2/3c. Blue Curacao
1/3c. Water

Tutti - Frutti

1c. Boiling Apple Juice
1 box Cherry Gelatin
1/4c. Peach Schnapps
3/8c. Gin
1/8c. Amaretto
1/4c. Water

Wapplemelon Wonder

1c. Boiling Water
1 box Watermelon Gelatin
1/3c. Watermelon Schnapps
1/3c. Sour Apple Schnapps
1/3c. Water

Watermelon Crawl

1c. Boiling Water
1 box Watermelon Gelatin
2/3c. Watermelon Schnapps
1/3c. Water

Index 1

This Index is arranged by Gelatin Type.

Index 2

This Index is arranged by Alcohol Type.

* Blue Curacao & Blue Schnapps can be substituted for one another

www.ingramcontent.com/pod-product-compliance
Ingram Content Group UK Ltd.
Pitfield, Milton Keynes, MK11 3LW, UK
UKHW041902190726
13854UKWH00003B/1040

9 781411 616950